Maccabee Meals

Food and Fun for
Hanukkah

Judye Groner &
Madeline Wikler

illustrated by
Ursula Roma

KAR-BEN
PUBLISHING

For our children, Josh, Ben, Judy and Karen, the inspiration for Kar-Ben, and for our grandchildren, our joy and our future.

— J.G. and M.W.

To Allison, Corinne, Karla, and all of my Jewish friends and relatives who have shared their food and rituals. Toda Raba!

— U.R.

KAR-BEN PUBLISHING
A division of Lerner Publishing Group, Inc.
241 First Avenue North
Minneapolis, MN 55401 U.S.A.
800-4KARBEN

Website address: www.karben.com

Library of Congress Cataloging-in-Publication Data

Groner, Judyth Saypol.
    Maccabee meals : food and fun for Hanukkah / by Judye Groner and Madeline Wikler ; illustrated by Ursula Roma.
        p.   cm.
    Includes index.
    ISBN: 978–0–7613–5144–3 (pbk. : alk. paper)
    1. Hanukkah cooking—Juvenile literature. 2. Cookbooks. I. Wikler, Madeline, 1943–
II. Roma, Ursula, ill. III. Title.
TX739.2.H35G76 2012
641.5′68—dc23   2011029020

Manufactured in the United States of America
1 – BP – 12/31/11

CONTENTS

The Story of
Hanukkah   4
Kitchen Tips   6

BRUNCH   9
Waffle Latkes with Yogurt
Candle Salad
Fruit Smoothie
Hanukkah Cookies
Fondue

AFTERNOON TEA   15
Cheese Coins
Cranberry Latkes
Tea Sandwiches
EZ Sufganiyot

SHABBAT DINNER   21
Cornflake Chicken
Traditional Latkes
Two Kinds of Applesauce
Grilled Root Vegetables
Sufganiyot

WINTER PICNIC   27
Hot Dog Mini-Kebabs
Coleslaw
Carrot Latkes
S'mores

OPEN HOUSE   33
Hero Sandwiches
Chicken Latkes
Menorah or Dreidel Cake

AFTER-SCHOOL
SNACKS   37
Cheese Latkes
Egg Cream
Alef-Bet Pretzels
Hanukkah Gelt
Trail Mix

PAJAMA PARTY   43
Apple Crunch Latkes
Cinnamon Toast
Chocolate Star Dreidels

ROSH CHODESH
TWILIGHT SUPPER   47
Tex-Mex Latkes
Guacamole
Burmuelos
Hot Spiced Milk
New Moon Cookies

Lighting the Candles   54
About the Dreidel   57
Hanukkah Decorations   59
Table Crafts   60
Party Etiquette   62
Index   63

The Story of Hanukkah

Long ago, the Jewish people lived in the land of Israel, then called Judea. They were ruled by the king of nearby Syria. Although they were not free, they were allowed to celebrate their holidays and pray in their holy temple in Jerusalem. But a new king, Antiochus, came to power. He forced the Jews to believe in Greek gods and to bow down to Greek statues. When some Jews refused, Antiochus sent soldiers to destroy the homes and Temple of the Jews.

In Modi'in, a town near Jerusalem, a man called Mattathias refused to bow down to the Greek statues. With his five sons, he fought off the soldiers and escaped to the nearby mountains. They organized a small army called the Maccabees, led by Mattathias's son Judah. Though they were few in number, and not well trained, the Maccabees were fighting for freedom, and their courage and skill enabled them to drive the Syrians away.

After three years of fighting, they reached Jerusalem. The Jewish fighters became builders, as they cleaned and rebuilt the Holy Temple. On the 25th day of the Hebrew month Kislev, they rekindled the lights of the menorah and rededicated the Holy Temple. Their celebration lasted eight days. Judah Maccabee and his brothers proclaimed that every year, for eight days, the Jews should celebrate a festival of lights. This holiday became known as Hanukkah.

There is a legend that the Maccabees were able to find only one jug of pure oil, enough to keep the Temple Menorah burning for only one day. But the oil lasted and lasted, and burned brightly for all eight days of the celebration.

KITCHEN TIPS

Before you begin...

1. Ask permission to use the kitchen.
2. If your recipe involves sharp knives, the stove, or other electrical appliances, make sure an adult is nearby to supervise.
3. Wash your hands and protect your clothes with an apron.
4. Read the recipe carefully and assemble all ingredients and equipment.
5. Keep a sponge or dish cloth handy for unexpected spills.

Safety Tips

1. Use potholders to handle hot dishes.
2. Pick up knives by the handles and always cut away from yourself.
3. Cooking with oil can be dangerous. Never, ever put out an oil fire with water. If you don't have a fire extinguisher, use salt, baking soda, or flour to suffocate the flames.

When You're Finished

Turn off the stove, put away all food and equipment, wipe the counters, and sweep the floor.

Remember, good cooks always leave the kitchen neat and clean.

USING THIS COOKBOOK

Meat/Dairy/Parve Symbols

 Meat recipe

 Dairy recipe

 Parve recipe – may be eaten with either meat or dairy

Degree of Difficulty

 No cooking or baking is required, and cutting may be done with a plastic knife.

 May require chopping or slicing, the use of a blender or food processor, and/or baking in the oven.

 A hot stove is used to boil or fry. An adult should be nearby to supervise.

METRIC CONVERSIONS

MASS (weight)

1 ounce (oz.) = 28 grams (g)
8 ounces = 227 g
1 pound (lb.) or 16 oz. = 0.45 kilograms (kg)
2.2 lbs. = 1 kg

LIQUID VOLUME

1 teaspoon (tsp.) = 5 milliliters (ml)
1 tablespoon (Tbsp.) = 15 ml
1 fluid ounce (oz.) = 30 ml
1 cup (c.) = 240 ml
1 pint (pt.) = 480 ml
1 quart (qt.) = 0.95 liters (l)
1 gallon (gal.) = 3.80 l

BRUNCH
Menu
Waffle Latkes with Yogurt
Candle Salad
Fruit Smoothie
Hanukkah Cookies
Fondue

Waffle Latkes with Yogurt

Ingredients

2 c. shredded potatoes (ready-made is fine)

1 small onion, diced

2 eggs

3 Tbsp. flour

½ tsp. baking powder

¼ c. oil

Salt and pepper to taste

1. Combine all ingredients in food processor until smooth.
2. Spoon into heated waffle iron and bake until golden brown.

Serves 4

Potato latkes are Hanukkah's signature dish, not because of the potato, but because of the oil. Potatoes did not exist in the Holy Land when the ancient Israelites triumphed over the Syrians. They are a relatively recent Eastern European tradition.

Candle Salad

Ingredients

2 lettuce leaves

½ c. cottage cheese

1 banana

2 canned pineapple rings

2 orange sections

1. Arrange each lettuce leaf on its own plate.
2. Top each with a small mound of cottage cheese, pineapple ring, and half a banana (cut side down).
3. Fasten orange section to the top with a toothpick for the candle flame.

Makes 2

Fruit Smoothie

Ingredients

1 c. plain or vanilla yogurt

1 c. milk

1 c. fresh or frozen fruit (banana, strawberries, peaches)

1 Tbsp. sugar or honey (optional)

Cut fruit into chunks, and combine all ingredients in blender until smooth.

Serves 2-3

Hanukkah Cookies

Ingredients

½ c. butter or margarine

1 c. sugar

1 tsp. vanilla

1 egg

1½ c. flour

1½ tsp. baking powder

¼ tsp. salt

1. Combine butter and sugar in bowl and beat until smooth.

2. Add egg and vanilla and mix well.

3. Mix flour, baking powder, and salt together in another bowl.

4. Gradually add dry ingredients to butter mixture. Add more flour if dough is too sticky.

5. Form dough into a ball, wrap in waxed paper, and chill for at least one hour.

6. Preheat oven to 375 degrees.

7. Roll out dough on floured surface. Cut with Hanukkah cookie cutters.

8. Bake on ungreased cookie sheet for 8-10 minutes until golden brown. Cool.

Makes 3-4 dozen

LATKE VS. HAMANTASCHEN

The Latke/Hamantaschen Debate, a spoof on Talmudic study, was first held in the winter of 1946, at the Hillel Foundation at the University of Chicago. Professors were invited to poke fun at scholarly life and Jewish tradition by arguing the relative merits of the two holiday treats.

For over six decades, the program has continued at the University of Chicago and has been copied by many campuses across the country. Academics from all disciplines have analyzed these foods from sociological, legal, artistic, nutritional, and economic perspectives.

Fondue

Ingredients

12 oz. bag of chocolate chips
1 c. light cream
½ tsp. vanilla

Dippers

Strawberries
Slices of banana, apple, pear
Pineapple chunks
Whole strawberries
Angel food or pound cake
Marshmallows

1. Melt chocolate in microwave or double-boiler.

2. Stir in cream and vanilla until smooth.

3. Transfer to chafing dish or fondue pot to keep warm.

4. Use long forks or skewers to dip fruit and cake in chocolate.

Caution: Cool before eating.

AFTERNOON TEA

Menu

Cheese Coins

Cranberry Latkes

Tea Sandwiches

EZ Sufganiyot

Cheese Coins

Ingredients

½ c. butter or margarine, softened

½ c. cheddar cheese, shredded

1 c. flour

1. Combine all ingredients in bowl. Mix well to form dough.

2. Divide in half and roll each half into a log. Wrap in waxed paper and chill or freeze for several hours or overnight.

3. Preheat oven to 375 degrees.

4. Unwrap cheese logs and slice into quarter inch thick coins.

5. Place an inch apart on ungreased cookie sheet.

6. Bake 10 minutes.

Makes 3-4 dozen

Hanukkah Gelt: In 1958, the Bank of Israel initiated a program of striking special commemorative coins for use as Hanukkah gelt. The first Hanukkah coin portrayed the same menorah that had appeared on the last Maccabean coins two centuries earlier. Each year the coin honors a different Jewish community around the world.

Cranberry Latkes

Ingredients

12 oz. bag cranberries

¾ c. water

1 c. raisins

½ c. orange juice

2 c. sugar

1 c. flour

2 eggs

Vegetable oil for frying

Whipped cream or non-dairy topping

1. In large pot simmer cranberries in water until they pop.

2. Add raisins, juice, and sugar, mixing well. Boil until mixture thickens (about 15 minutes). Cool.

3. Stir in flour and eggs.

4. Heat oil in large frying pan over low flame. Drop batter by tablespoons and flatten with back of spoon. As latkes can burn easily, turn often until both sides are lightly browned and still soft.

5. Drain on paper towels. Serve with whipped topping.

Tea Sandwiches

Menorah Sandwich

Ingredients

1 slice of bread

Whipped cream cheese, plain or flavored

8 small pretzel sticks

1 carrot stick

9 raisins

1. Spread cream cheese on bread.

2. Line up pretzel stick "candles" and carrot stick "shamash" to make a menorah.

3. Use raisins to "light" your menorah.

Serves 1

Star Sandwich

Ingredients
2 slices bread
Peanut butter and jelly

1. Make a peanut butter and jelly sandwich and cut off crusts.
2. Cut sandwich in half diagonally. Crisscross the halves to form a 6-pointed star.

Serves 1

Pinwheel Sandwiches

Ingredients
Soft tortilla
Cheese spread
Fresh spinach leaves

1. Spread cheese and spinach on tortilla. Roll up.
2. Wrap in waxed paper and chill for one hour or more.
3. Slice into pinwheels.

EZ Sufganiyot

Ingredients

1 package of refrigerator biscuits, thawed
½ c. butter, melted
Sugar and cinnamon mixture

1. Pull apart the biscuits and punch a hole in the middle.
2. Roll in melted butter, then in cinnamon mixture.
3. Bake according to package directions.

The first Hanukkah postage stamp was issued jointly by the U.S. government and the State of Israel in 1996. Designed by Washington DC artist Hannah Smotrich, the stamp featured a multicolored array of candles created from cut paper.

In 2004, a new stamp was issued. It was a photograph of an Israeli dreidel made by Elise Moore with "Hanukkah" spelled out in creative type designed by Greg Berger.

A third stamp, issued in 2009, features a photograph of a menorah designed by Lisa Reagan and photographed by Ira Wexler.

SHABBAT DINNER

Menu

Cornflake Chicken

Traditional Latkes

Two Kinds of Applesauce

Grilled Root Vegetables

Sufganiyot

Cornflake Chicken

Ingredients

3 lbs. chicken pieces
1 c. Italian dressing
1–2 c. cornflake crumbs

1. Marinate chicken in Italian dressing for at least one hour.

2. Preheat oven to 375 degrees.

3. Put crumbs in a paper bag and add chicken pieces. Toss until covered.

4. Spray cookie sheet with oil or line with foil. Bake for 45 minute to 1 hour depending on the size of the pieces.

Serves 4-6

In the shtetls (villages) of Eastern Europe, roast goose was a Hanukkah delicacy. Families raised their own geese, and housewives would begin to fatten them up in the fall. The feathers were used for pillows and comforters, and the fat was rendered and used for cooking.

Traditional Latkes

Ingredients

4 medium potatoes (about 4 c.)
  (Russet potatoes work well)
1 tsp. vinegar
1 medium onion, diced (about ½ c.)
2 eggs
2 tsp. salt
2 Tbsp. matzah meal or flour
Oil for frying

1. Peel potatoes (optional). If you don't peel them, wash them well.
2. Grate or shred in processor. Drain excess liquid. Sprinkle vinegar on top to keep potatoes from discoloring.
3. Add rest of ingredients and mix thoroughly.
4. Heat ⅛ inch of oil in large frying pan. Carefully place spoonfuls of batter into hot oil and fry on both sides until brown. Drain on paper towels.

If you wish to make these ahead, they may be reheated in hot oven on cookie sheets lined with brown paper.

Cooked Applesauce

Ingredients

8 medium or 6 large apples (a mixture of tart and sweet)

½ c. water

Dash of salt

½ c. sugar

½ tsp. cinnamon

1. Peel and core apples.

2. Put in pot with water and salt. Bring to a boil and simmer until apples are soft (about 30 minutes). Alternatively, place in microwave-safe bowl and cover. Microwave until apples are soft (10-15 minutes).

3. Stir in sugar and cinnamon. Serve warm or cold.

No-Cook Applesauce

Ingredients

4 large apples

½ c. water

3 Tbsp. honey

¼ tsp. cinnamon

1. Peel, core, and slice apples into large chunks.

2. Place in blender or processor with rest of ingredients and blend until smooth. You may have to do this in several batches. Serve immediately.

Grilled Root Vegetables

Ingredients

3 c. root vegetables (pick from: carrots, parsnips, sweet
potatoes, onions, rutabagas, beets, turnips, garlic)
2–3 Tbsp. vegetable oil
Salt and pepper
Spices to taste (cumin, thyme, rosemary)

1. Preheat oven to 375 degrees.

2. Peel and cut vegetables into one-inch chunks.

3. Toss in olive oil and spread on cookie sheet.

4. Sprinkle with salt, pepper, and spices.

5. Roast for 45 minutes to one hour or until soft inside and lightly browned.

Serves 3-4

Note: Beets will turn everything pink. You may want to roast them separately.

Sufganiyot

Ingredients

½ c. orange juice
¼ c. margarine or butter
4 Tbsp. sugar
2 packages dry yeast
3-4 c. flour
2 eggs, beaten
Dash of salt
Oil for frying
Powdered sugar

1. Combine juice, margarine, and sugar. Heat or microwave to melt margarine. Cool to lukewarm.

2. Add yeast, 3 c. flour and beaten eggs. Knead until smooth, adding more flour if necessary. Cover with damp dishtowel and let rise for 30 minutes.

3. Punch down, divide into portions the size of a golf ball. Shape into balls, rings, or braids. Let rise another 30 minutes.

4. Heat I c. oil in frying pan. Fry donuts, turning to brown on all sides. Remove with slotted spoon and drain on paper towel.

5. Put powdered sugar in paper bag, add donuts, and shake to cover.

Serves 6-8

Israelis eat an average of three sufganiyot per person during Hanukkah. Some years sales have topped 20,000,000. In addition to the traditional jelly fillings, popular flavors include chocolate, butterscotch, coffee, pistachio, halva, and lemon meringue.

WINTER PICNIC

Menu

Hot Dog Mini-Kebabs
Coleslaw
Carrot Latkes
S'mores

Hot Dog Mini-Kebabs

Ingredients

2 hot dogs
10 cherry tomatoes
Pickle slices
Mustard and ketchup
Toothpicks

1. Cook or grill hot dogs. Slice into one-inch rounds.

2. Alternate hot dog, tomato, and pickle slice on toothpicks. Serve with mustard and ketchup.

Makes 20

MODI'IN TORCH RELAY

As Hanukkah begins, thousands of young people gather at Modi'in, the ancient home of the Maccabees. A large bonfire is lit, torches are kindled, and runners carry them in relay to every city and farm in Israel.

Coleslaw

Ingredients

1 bag of shredded coleslaw mix
½ c. vinegar
1 Tbsp. sugar
½ c. mayonnaise
Salt and pepper to taste

1. Marinate cole slaw mix in vinegar and sugar for one hour or more.

2. Add mayonnaise and season to taste.

The first day of Hanukkah and Christmas Day
coincide once every 38 years. It last happened in
1978 and will happen again in 2016.

Carrot Latkes

Ingredients

2 c. grated carrots (6-8 carrots)

1 medium onion, grated

3 eggs

½ c. matzah meal

½ tsp. baking powder

Salt and pepper to taste

Oil for frying

1. Combine carrots and onion in large bowl. Add rest of ingredients and mix thoroughly.

2. Heat ⅛ inch of oil in large frying pan.

3. Carefully place spoonfuls of batter into hot oil and fry on both sides until brown.

4. Drain on paper towels.

Makes 10-12

S'mores

Ingredients

Graham crackers

Chocolate bar, broken into squares

Marshmallows

1. Preheat oven to 350 degrees.

2. Line baking sheet with foil or parchment.

3. Place graham crackers on cookie sheet and top each with a square of chocolate and a marshmallow. Bake for 4-5 minutes until marshmallows melt and chocolate softens.

4. Remove from oven and top each s'more with another graham cracker to make a sandwich.

OPEN HOUSE

Menu

Hero Sandwiches

Chicken Latkes

Menorah or Dreidel Cake

Hero Sandwiches

Ingedients

Sandwich roll

Assorted cold cuts – salami, bologna, pastrami, corned beef, turkey

Toppings such as mustard, ketchup, pickles, onions, lettuce, tomato

1. Slice roll in half lengthwise and spread with desired condiments.
2. Add meats and toppings. Slice into serving portions.

Chicken Latkes

Ingredients

1 lb. cooked chicken, diced

½ c. onion, chopped

2 eggs, beaten

½ c. matzah meal

Salt and pepper to taste

Oil for frying

1. Saute onion in oil. In bowl, combine chicken, eggs, and matzah meal. Add sautéed onions. Season to taste.
2. Heat ⅛ inch of oil in large frying pan.
3. Carefully place spoonfuls of batter into hot oil and fry on both sides until brown.
4. Drain on paper towels.

Serves 3-4

34

Hanukkat Habayit

The custom of rededication, which began with the rededication of the Holy Temple by the Maccabees, is one that continues to this day. Because the Jewish home is the center of so much of Jewish life and celebration, it is often referred to as a mikdash m'at, a little temple. When we move into a new house, it is customary to have a hanukkat ha-bayit, which begins with the fastening of a mezuzah to the doorpost of the house.

Menorah or Dreidel Cake

Ingredients

1 package of cake mix
1 package of frosting mix or can of frosting
Orange or lemon candies

1. Prepare cake according to package directions and bake in a 9 x 13 inch pan.
2. Cool cake, remove from pan, wrap in foil, and freeze.
3. Remove from freezer and unwrap. Let thaw slightly while you prepare frosting.
4. Cut cake into pieces as shown to make a dreidel or menorah. Assemble pieces on cookie sheet or tray and frost while cake is still partially frozen.
5. Use candy drops for candle flames on menorah or to make a letter on the dredel.

Serves 8-10

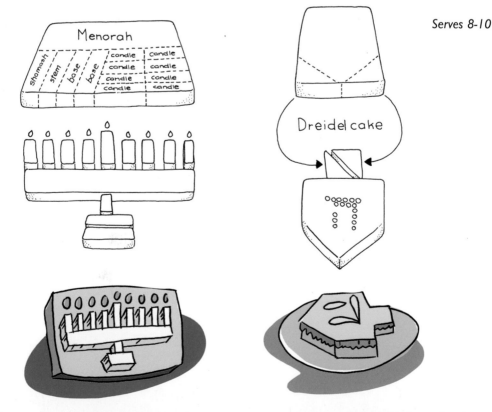

AFTER-SCHOOL SNACKS

Menu

Cheese Latkes

Egg Cream

Alef-Bet Pretzels

Hanukkah Gelt

Trail Mix

THE LEGEND OF JUDITH

Latkes were originally made with cheese, recalling the legend of Judith.
When General Holofernes threatened the Jews, Judith fed him salty cheese
so that he would drink lots of wine to quench his thirst. When he was drunk,
she cut off his head, giving the Jews a victory over the Assyrians.

Cheese Latkes

Ingredients

1 c. ricotta cheese

4 eggs

⅔ c. flour

½ tsp. salt

Oil for frying

Sour cream

1. Put cheese and eggs in bowl and mix well.

2. Add flour and salt and mix again.

3. Heat ⅛ inch of oil in large frying pan.

4. Carefully place spoonfuls of batter into hot oil and fry on both sides until brown.

5. Drain on paper towels. Serve with sour cream.

Serves 3-4

Egg Cream

Ingredients

16 oz. bottle of club soda, chilled

1 c. milk

¼ c. chocolate syrup

4 glasses and straws

1. Put 1 Tbsp. chocolate syrup and ¼ milk in each of 4 glasses.

2. Fill slowly to the top with club soda. Serve with straws.

Serves 4

Alef–Bet Pretzels

Ingredients

1 pkg. dry yeast
1 c. warm water
3 c. flour
1 Tbsp. sugar
1 tsp. salt
1 egg, beaten with 1 Tbsp. water
Kosher salt
Margarine or oil spray

1. In a bowl, dissolve yeast in water.

2. Add flour, sugar, and salt and work into a dough.

3. Cover with a towel and let rise 1 hour.

4. Preheat oven to 425 degrees.

5. Grease cookie sheet.

6. Divide dough into pieces the size of a golf ball. Dust hands with flour. Roll dough into sausages and shape into the letters on the dreidel.

7. Place on cookie sheet, brush with egg mixture, and sprinkle with salt.

8. Bake for 25 minutes or until brown.

Hanukkah Gelt

Ingredients

3 c. semi-sweet chocolate chips

1 can sweetened condensed milk

1 tsp. vanilla

¼ tsp. salt

Waxed paper and foil

1. Combine chocolate chips and condensed milk in microwaveable bowl and heat for one minute. Stir. If chocolate is not melted, continue heating in microwave for 10 seconds at a time until mixture is smooth.

2. Add vanilla and salt and stir.

3. Line a baking pan with waxed paper.

4. Spread mixture evenly in pan. Refrigerate for ½ hour.

5. Using the top of a spice bottle or other small circle, cut fudge into rounds and wrap in foil.

TRAIL MIX

Ingredients

1½ c. old-fashioned oats (not instant)

1 c. mixed nuts (almonds, walnuts, pecans, peanuts)

¼ c. sunflower seeds

½ c. dried fruits (berries, apricots, apples, etc.)

Mix together:

¼ c. vegetable oil

1 tsp. vanilla

¼ c. honey

Dash of cinnamon (optional)

1. Pour liquid mixture over dry mixture and spread onto a cookie sheet.

2. Bake at 375 degrees for 20 to 30 minutes, stirring once or twice. Cool and break up any lumps.

PAJAMA PARTY

Menu

Apple Crunch Latkes
Cinnamon Toast
Chocolate Star Dreidels

Apple Crunch Latkes

Ingredients

1 c. pancake mix

1 c. apple juice

1 egg

½ c. chopped apples

¼ c. raisins

¼ c. chopped nuts

Cinnamon and sugar

1. Combine all ingredients.
2. Heat ⅛ inch of oil in large frying pan.
3. Carefully place spoonfuls of batter into hot oil and fry on both sides until brown.
4. Drain on paper towels. Serve with cinnamon and sugar.

Serves 3-4

HANUKKAH MIDRASH

As winter approached, Adam watched the days grow shorter and the nights grow longer. He began to worry that he had done something wrong and that he was being punished. So he fasted and prayed for eight days. When the winter solstice arrived, he noticed the days were getting longer again. He recognized that this was part of the cycle of seasons and not a punishment. Adam decided that to show his appreciation to God, from then on he would mark the solstice with an eight-day festival.

— Talmud Avodah Zarah 8a

Cinnamon Toast

Ingredients

2 slices of bread
1 Tbsp. butter or margarine
Mixture of ¼ tsp. cinnamon, 1 Tbsp. sugar

1. Spread bread slices with butter or margarine and sprinkle with cinnamon-sugar mixture.
2. Brown in toaster oven or under broiler until sugar bubbles.

Serves 2

Chocolate Star Dreidels

Ingredients

12 marshmallows
12 chocolate stars or kisses
Peanut butter
12 1-inch long pieces of licorice or other candy stick
Toothpicks
Food coloring

1. Spread peanut butter on one side of marshmallow and attach chocolate kiss.
2. Poke the licorice or candy stick into the marshmallow for a handle.
3. Dip a toothpick in food coloring and paint a dreidel letter on the marshmallow.

Makes 12

ROSH CHODESH TWILIGHT SUPPER

Menu

Tex-Mex Latkes

Guacamole

Burmuelos

Hot Spiced Milk

New Moon Cookies

Tex-Mex Latkes

Ingredients

2 c. grated potatoes

2 eggs

2 tsp. lemon juice

2 Tbsp. chopped parsley or cilantro

¼ c. chopped scallions

¼ c. flour

Salt and pepper to taste

Oil for frying

½ c. grated cheese (optional)

Salsa

1. Mix first 7 ingredients together in a bowl.
2. Heat ⅛ inch of oil in large frying pan.
3. Carefully place spoonfuls of batter into hot oil and fry on both sides until brown.
4. Drain on paper towels.
5. Top with grated cheese (optional) and serve with salsa.

Serves 3-4

Hanukkah is the only Jewish holiday celebrated in two different Hebrew months. It begins on the 25th day of Kislev and continues until the 2nd day of the month of Tevet.

HANUKKAH MOON

Rosh Chodesh Tevet, the new moon of the Hebrew month Tevet, always falls during the eight days of Hanukkah. It is the new moon closest to the Winter Solstice and spans the darkest time of the year.

According to legend, because women refused to contribute their jewelry toward the building of the Golden Calf, they were rewarded with the monthly holiday of Rosh Chodesh. Today, women have created candlelighting ceremonies and prayers to usher in the new moon each month. Sephardim, Jews who trace their ancestors back to Spain and Portugal, have special celebrations on the Rosh Chodesh that falls during Hanukkah.

Guacamole

Ingredients

2 ripe avocados, mashed
1 small onion, finely chopped
1 clove garlic, minced
1 ripe tomato, chopped
Juice of a lime
Salt and pepper to taste

1. Mash avocados in bowl with rest of ingredients. Chill to blend flavors.
2. Serve with sliced veggies. Makes 2 cups.

Burmuelos

Ingredients

2 eggs
½ c. melted butter or margarine
I Tbsp. sugar
I tsp. vanilla
¾ c. milk
3 c. flour
I Tbsp. baking powder
I tsp. salt
Cinnamon-sugar mixture
Oil for frying

1. Beat together eggs, butter, sugar, and vanilla.

2. Stir in milk.

3. Add dry ingredients.

4. Form into dough, knead, and shape into small balls. Cover and let stand for ½ hour.

5. Roll balls out into thin circles.

6. Heat 2 inches of oil in frying pan until hot. Fry circles until golden brown on both sides.

7. Drain on paper towels. Sprinkle with cinnamon and sugar.

Hot Spiced Milk

Ingredients
12 oz. milk
2½ tsp. light brown sugar
⅛ tsp. cinnamon
⅛ tsp. vanilla
Small pinch salt
Cocoa powder and/or cinnamon

1. Combine first five ingredients, and warm over low heat in microwave or on stovetop.
2. Sprinkle with cocoa powder or cinnamon.
3. Pour into mugs.

Serves 2

New Moon Cookies

Ingredients
1 c. butter or margarine
½ c. sugar
½ c. ground almonds
1¼ c. flour
¼ tsp. salt

1. Preheat oven to 325 degrees.
2. Cream sugar and butter. Adds nuts, flour, and salt.
3. Form into dough and chill one hour or more.
4. Roll small pieces of dough into sausage shapes and curve into crescents.
5. Bake on ungreased cookie sheet for 15 minutes. Sprinkle with powdered sugar if desired.

Makes 2 dozen

THE VERSATILE OLIVE

Olive trees grow easily in the rocky, sandy soil of Israel, and from Biblical times they provided food, fuel, and wood. Olive oil was used for cooking, anointing the body during religious ceremonies, and lighting lamps such as the menorah in the Temple.

LIGHTING THE CANDLES

The Hanukkah menorah, called the hanukkiyah, should be lit at sunset and placed in front of a window so that people passing by can see the candles burning. You need 44 candles for all eight nights. Each night a shamash (helper) candle is lit and is used to light first one candle, then two, and so forth.

Candles should be lined up from right to left. The last candle added is the first one lit, and lighting continues from left to right.

In some families, it is the custom for everyone to light his or her own hanukkiyah. In other families, parents and children take turns.

On Shabbat, the Hanukkah candles are lit before the Shabbat candles. At the end of Shabbat, Hanukkah candles are lit after Havdallah.

Israel's national emblem combines the seven-branch menorah that stood in the Holy Temple and the olive branch, the symbol of peace.

THE GREAT DEBATE

The Hebrew letters of the word Hanukkah are an acronym for the phrase Chet Nerot K'halacha K'bet Hillel (eight candles according to the ruling of Bet Hillel).

In Rabbinic times, the famous schools of Hillel and Shammai debated the order of lighting the Hanukkah candles. Shammai's followers held that eight candles should be lit the first night and one fewer each succeeding night, representing the gradual depletion of the little jug of pure oil. Hillel's students believed we should begin with a single candle and add one each night because the symbol of holiness should grow. The school of Hillel prevailed, and we follow his order today.

CANDLE BLESSINGS

בָּרוּךְ אַתָּה יְיָ אֱלֹהֵינוּ מֶלֶךְ הָעוֹלָם אֲשֶׁר קִדְּשָׁנוּ בְּמִצְוֹתָיו וְצִוָּנוּ לְהַדְלִק נֵר שֶׁל חֲנֻכָּה.

Baruch Atah Adonai Eloheinu melech ha'olam asher kideshanu b'mitzvotav v' tzivanu l' hadlik ner shel Hanukkah.

We praise you, Adonai our God, Ruler of the World, who makes us holy by Your mitzvot and commands us to light the Hanukkah candles.

בָּרוּךְ אַתָּה יְיָ אֱלֹהֵינוּ מֶלֶךְ הָעוֹלָם שֶׁעָשָׂה נִסִּים לַאֲבוֹתֵינוּ בַּיָּמִים הָהֵם בַּזְּמַן הַזֶּה.

Baruch Atah Adonai Eloheinu melech ha'olam she' asah nisim la' avoteinu bayamim hahem baz' man hazeh.

We praise you, Adonai our God, Ruler of the World, who made miracles for our ancestors in those days.

On the first night we add a third blessing:

בָּרוּךְ אַתָּה יְיָ אֱלֹהֵינוּ מֶלֶךְ הָעוֹלָם שֶׁהֶחֱיָנוּ וְקִיְּמָנוּ וְהִגִּיעָנוּ לַזְּמַן הַזֶּה.

Baruch Atah Adonai Eloheinu melech ha'olam shehecheyanu, v' kiyemanu, v' higianu, lazman hazeh.

We praise you, Adonai our God, Ruler of the World, who has kept us alive and well so that we can celebrate this special time.

ABOUT THE DREIDEL

The dreidel is a spinning top. Its name in Yiddish means "turn."
The Hebrew word for dreidel is sevivon, which also means "turn."
There are four letters on the dreidel :

נ **Nun**

ג **Gimel**

ה **Hey**

ש **Shin**

They stand for the words Nes Gadol Hayah Sham, which means
"A Great Miracle Happened There."

Dreidels in Israel have different letters:

נ **Nun**

ג **Gimel**

ה **Hey**

פ **Pey**

They stand for the words Nes Gadol Haya Po, which means
"A Great Miracle Happened Here."

DREIDEL TRIVIA

The four sides of the dreidel symbolize four empires that once enslaved the
Jewish people—Babylonia, Persia, Greece, and Rome.

In gematria (mystical numerology) the sum of the letters on the dreidel
(nun, gimmel, hey, and shin) total 358. This is the same as the word nachash
(the serpent that seduced Adam and Eve) and mashiach (messiah). The dreidel
represents the toppling of evil and the wish for the messianic era.

HOW TO PLAY DREIDEL

HERE ARE THE RULES FOR PLAYING DREIDEL:

Everyone starts with an equal number of pennies, nuts, raisins, or Hanukkah gelt.

Each player puts one of these in the middle. The first player spins the dreidel. If it lands on:

נ **Nun**—The player does nothing.

ג **Gimel**—The player takes everything in the pot.

ה **Hey**—The player takes half.

ש **Shin**—The player puts one in.

In Israel, if you land on a **פ** **(Pey)** you also put one in.

DREIDEL VARIATIONS

1. See who can keep a dreidel spinning the longest. Time the spins with a stop-watch.

2. Try spinning the dreidel upside down.

3. Let everyone spin a dreidel at the same time. Those whose dreidels land on the same letter get a point. Play to a specified number of points.

4. Hebrew letters stand for numbers:

נ **Nun—50**

ג **Gimel—3**

ה **Hey—5**

ש **Shin—300**

פ **Pey—80**

Take turns spinning the dreidel and record each player's score. See who can get to 1,000 first.

DECORATIONS

SPINNING DREIDELS

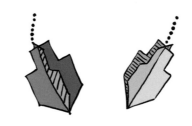

You will need:

   Construction paper

   Scissors, hole punch, string

1. Put two pieces of construction paper together, fold them in half, and draw half a dreidel shape along the fold. Cut them out.

2. Slit each dreidel along the fold: one halfway from the top to the center, and the other halfway from the bottom to the center. Slide the two together through the slits.

3. Punch a small hole in the top and hang your spinning dreidels around the room. You may make spinning candles and stars the same way.

HANUKKAH CHAIN

You will need:

   Construction paper

   Scissors, scotch tape or stapler, pencil, markers or crayons

1. Cut strips of construction paper and link together to form a paper chain.

2. Draw Hanukkah symbols (dreidels, candles, menorahs, gelt, Judah Maccabee, jug of oil) and cut them out, leaving a strip at the top to loop over and attach to your chain.

TABLE CRAFTS

PLACECARDS

You will need:

    Construction paper

    Drinking straws

    Scissors, markers, hole punch

1. Draw small dreidel shapes and cut them out.

2. Write your guests' names on each and decorate.

3. Punch holes near the top and bottom and push a straw through the holes.

4. Put each dreidel placecard in a cup when you set your table.

PLACEMATS

You will need:

    Labels from candle boxes and Hanukkah food, wrapping paper,
      colorful Hanukkah ads

    Shirt cardboard or heavy construction paper

    Clear self-adhesive shelf paper

    Scissors, glue

1. Cut out pieces of labels, ads, and wrapping paper in a variety of shapes and arrange in a collage on a sheet of construction paper. When you're happy with your design, glue all the shapes to the paper.

2. Cover both sides with clear, adhesive paper.

The placemats may be wiped clean and stored for future holiday meals.

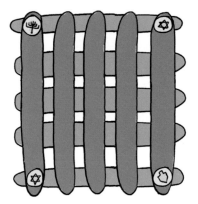

HOT PLATE

You will need:
   10 popsicle sticks
   Felt or construction paper
   Scissors, glue

1. Put glue across five popsicle sticks. Space the dry sticks across the five glued ones.

2. Cut out Hanukkah shapes from felt or construction paper and place them on the corners of your hot plate.

ORIGAMI CUPS

You will need:
   Squares of thin paper (7 or 8 inches)—wrapping paper works well
   Scissors, marker

1. Fold your square into a triangle, with the folded edge on the bottom.

2. Now fold each bottom corner of the triangle upward to meet the opposite edge.

3. Tuck the top front flap into the open fold and the top back flap into the cup.

4. Spread open carefully and fill.

Use your cups to hold pennies, buttons, raisins, or nuts to play dreidel. Note: they won't hold liquid!

PARTY ETIQUETTE

Etiquette is a French word meaning "rules of good behavior." Here are a few rules to remember, whether you are the party giver or a party guest.

PARTY GIVER

1. Plan your party. Decide on your invitations, menu, decorations, and any games you will play.

2. E-mail or send your invitations at least ten days before your party. Don't hand out invitations in school unless you plan to invite your whole class.

3. Check to see if any guests have any food allergies or special needs.

4. Introduce your guests to each other and to your family. If some of your guests don't know each other, you may want to provide name tags.

5. Thank your guests for coming and your family for helping you.

6. Make sure to clean up after your party.

7. If anyone brings a gift, make sure to send a thank-you note.

PARTY GUEST

1. Be sure to answer a party invitation promptly, so the party giver can plan.

2. Arrive on time and arrange to be picked up on time.

3. Be friendly, especially to anyone you don't know.

4. Respect the home you are visiting. A well-behaved guest is a welcome guest.

5. If you have any food restrictions, make sure you tell your host ahead of time. If you are served a food you dislike, just say, "no thank you." Don't make a fuss or a face.

6. When you leave, make sure to thank your host.

Maccabee Meals Index

Latkes

Apple Crunch Latkes	44
Carrot Latkes	31
Chicken Latkes	34
Cranberry Latkes	17
Potato Latkes	23
Tex-Mex Latkes	48
Waffle Latkes	10

Desserts and Sweets

Alef-Bet Pretzels	40
Burmuelos	51
Chocolate Star Dreidels	46
EZ Sufganiyot	20
Fondue	14
Hanukkah Cookies	12
Hanukkah Gelt	41
Menorah/Dreidel Cake	36
New Moon Cookies	52
S'mores	32
Sufganiyot	26
Trail Mix	42

Main Dishes

Candle Salad	11
Cheese Coins	16
Cheese Latkes	39
Cinnamon Toast	46
Cornflake Chicken	22
Hero Sandwiches	34
Hot Dog Mini-Kebabs	28
Tea Sandwiches	18

Drinks

Egg Cream	39
Fruit Smoothie	11
Hot Spiced Milk	52

Sides

Applesauce	24
Cole Slaw	30
Grilled Vegetables	25
Guacamole	50

Judye Groner and **Madeline Wikler** founded Kar-Ben Copies, Inc. in 1975, with the publication of *My Very Own Haggadah*, which they wrote and illustrated. The book has sold over 2 million copies and is still in print. They have authored more than two dozen books, as well as 36 editions of *My Very Own Jewish Calendar*, and have received the prestigious *Sydney Taylor Body of Work Award* from the Association of Jewish Libraries. They are the Editorial Directors of Kar-Ben Publishing, acquired by Lerner Publishing Group in 2001.

Ursula Roma is a fine artist, illustrator, and graphic designer who loves making art night and day. She also loves nature, animals, and kind people.